SCARS

Written by Susan Foley, M.D.
and Regen Foley

The Sunshine Project Inc.

Special Thanks to:

SFRO

SOUTH FLORIDA
RADIATION ONCOLOGY

The Sunshine Project Inc.

For making the publication of this book possible.

Production Date: 08/01/12
Printed by Everbest Printing (Guangzhou, China), Co. Ltd
Batch #: 109532

Layout and Cover Design by Jared Stevens

ISBN: 978-0-9848289-1-3

Scars are marks on your body that form when the skin heals from an injury or surgery.

Everyone has a scar!
Your belly button is a scar.
It is where you were connected to your mother
before you were born to get oxygen and nutrition.

There are many ways
to get scars:

Operations   Accidents
Burns   Sores
Birthmarks   Skin conditions
Infections   Medical treatments
Injuries (cuts and scrapes)

Many people get scars.

Each year in the United States there are:

2,900,000 injuries from car accidents

1,500,000 people diagnosed with a new cancer

450,000 people treated for burns

100,000 gunshot wounds

120,000 babies born with birth defects

46,000,000 surgeries

If you have scars you are not alone.

Scars can occur anywhere
on your body.

Some scars can be seen all the time.
Clothes hide some scars.

In some cultures scars are
intentionally made on a person's face or body.

These scars might stand for power, beauty, or wealth.
They can also identify a person as a member
of a certain tribe.

Many famous people have scars.

They are
beautiful,
handsome,
successful,
strong,
and happy.

Anyone can get scars.
Most people have a few
scars somewhere
on their body.

You don't get scars because you are bad.

They are not a punishment.

Scars are a natural result of your body healing itself.

Scars can represent:

Courage

Struggle for life

Beating a disease

A battle fought and won

Survival

Sometimes scars are the result of great bravery, such as:
Soldiers fighting for freedom
People battling cancer
Surviving a serious surgery or illness

Many people have surgery or receive medical treatment knowing it will give them scars. That does not keep them from getting the treatment they need.

Scars can hurt, ache, or be very sensitive to touch.

Even your clothes lightly brushing over
a scar might bother you.

The area around the scar might feel like it is pulling.
As the skin heals it might feel itchy.

Your doctor might tell you to be very careful that no
one bumps your scars for several
weeks or months.

That gives scars time to
heal and get strong.

Over time the pain gets better or even goes away.
The feeling of pulling or itching also goes away.
One day you might suddenly realize that your scars
don't bother you anymore!

The way scars look changes over time.
At first scars usually look thick and red.
They might feel hard.
Over months the color usually fades and they
get flatter and softer.
It might take many months or even a year for
your scars to completely heal.
Usually scars look better and feel better over time.
Small scars can even disappear.

If you have any questions about your scars and how they look or feel, it is best to ask your doctor.

It can be frightening to get scars,
especially at first.

In the beginning most people feel very sad.
You might also feel:
angry, confused, or embarrassed.

How you feel about your scars
depends on a lot of things:

- how big they are
- where they are located on your body
- how old you were when you got them
- how long ago you got the scars
- how it happened
- how you feel about yourself
- how your friends and family react
- how much support you have and having someone to talk to about it

Your feelings about your scars change over time.
This is the path that some people's feelings take:

Unhappy

Acceptance

Feeling that
your scars give
you individuality

How you feel about your scars
can even change from day to day.

Some people have a hard time
adjusting to their scars.

They take a long time to feel better.

Other people are more resilient.
That means they adjust in a positive way
to even difficult things.

Some people think
they are ugly because
of their scars.

Some people feel
ashamed of their
scars.

There is no need to be ashamed or to feel ugly.
Scars are beautiful and make you unique.

It is normal to worry about how people
will react to your scars.

Some people might try
to be polite and ignore
your scars.

Other people stare,
which may make you
feel uncomfortable.

People are curious
and may ask
questions.

They might ask
how you got the
scars or if they hurt.

Some people feel
afraid when they
see scars.

A few people might make fun of you.
They may tease you because they are
fearful or ignorant.

How you handle questions about your scars
depends on how you feel about them.

How much you say is up to you.
If you want to you can tell people what happened.
But you don't need to say anything if you
don't feel like sharing.

It is good to have something in mind to tell people.
You can practice what you want to say.
A parent, friend, counselor, or your doctor might help
you think of some answers.

Here are some things you could say:

"I was in a bad accident and this is where I was hurt."

"This scar is where I had an operation that saved my life."

"I don't feel like talking about it."

"It used to hurt but it doesn't anymore."

What you say might change how people treat you and how they treat other people with scars.

How you react might affect how you feel about yourself.

At first it will be hard to talk to people about your scars, but over time it becomes easier. Some people may never understand how you feel about your scars, and that is ok.

These are things that make you feel better:

Time
Most people feel better as time passes.

Acceptance by other people

Talking to other people with scars and realizing
that you are not alone

Reaching out to other people to help them cope
with their scars

Talking to your doctors might help.
You can tell them how you feel and ask questions.
You might want to ask what to expect from your scars.

You can also talk to a counselor about your feelings.

Something else that may make you feel better is knowing you are still strong and beautiful.

Maybe even
STRONGER and MORE beautiful.

This might be hard to believe but
over time you might learn that getting
scars isn't all bad!!!

Many people learn and grow from getting scars.
The experience of getting scars can teach empathy.
It can make you more understanding of other people.

Scars might change you to be a "deeper,"
more thoughtful person.

It might make you better able to handle
life events in the future.

With time most people accept their scars.

Scars become part of who you are and give
you individuality.
They show you have courage.

Scars are a symbol of survival.
Embrace your scars.

Embrace someone you know who has scars.
Honor their courage.

ABOUT THE AUTHORS

Susan Foley, M.D., F.A.A.P., is a board certified pediatrician who lives and works in South Florida. Involved in many non-profit organizations that serve the welfare and mental health of children and families, she served on the board of several of these organizations. Her husband died of cancer in 1998. She found few resources available to help her daughter at this difficult time, so together they wrote their first book, Close to my Heart, to help other children faced with the death of a loved one. The success of that book inspired them to write other books for children that tackle difficult issues.

Regen Foley, a graduate of Tulane University, is currently a graduate student at Georgetown University. She has been involved in community service all of her life. Regen lost her beloved stepfather to cancer on her tenth birthday. In his honor she founded and runs her own non- profit organization, The Sunshine Project, Inc. [a 501(c)(3)]. She survived a life threatening illness herself at the age of fifteen.